Radical
PRAYER

Radical PRAYER

Transform Your Life and the World in 28 Days

BY ANNIE BOTTICELLI

LUMINOUS LIFE
PUBLISHING
Books & Beyond

Venice, Florida, USA
www.LuminousLifePublishing.com
Luminous Life Publishing is a division of Annie Helps You, LLC.

For more information contact the author through
www.AnnieHelpsYou.com

ISBN: 978-1-68454-074-7 (paperback)
    978-1-68454-072-3 (epub)

Acknowledgements

I honor with the deepest gratitude those master teachers whose work has supported me through massive transformation. Special thanks to David Daniel Kennedy, Don Miguel Ruiz, Wayne Dyer, Louise Hay, Melody Beattie, Michael Brown, Florence Shovel Shinn, Leslie Temple Thurston and Brad Laughlin, Margaret Lynch, Dr. C. Norm Shealy, Jan Spiller, and the Ho'Oponopono. I am so grateful for the bodies of work they created to help support me and others through the wild journey of Conscious Evolution.

THANK YOU, INFINITE SPIRIT, FOR
ALLOWING ME TO BE A CHANNEL
OF YOUR LIGHT & LOVE.

I AM SO EXCITED AND GRATEFUL
TO PLAY MY PIECE IN THE GREAT
SYMPHONY OF LIFE.

Table of Contents

About the
Author

Annie Botticelli is an Internationally-Renowned Youtube Personality, Astrologer, Author, Blogger, Singer, Radical Self-Development Coach, Trainer of Astrologers and Coaches, Founder of and Teacher at her Online Schools: Shine Your Brilliance Vocational University, Astaria School of Practical Magic, and Luminous Life Multiversity, Founder & Alchemist at Consciousness Blossoms ~ Organic Bath & Body Products, Founder of Luminous Life Publishing ~ Books & Beyond, Sweet Starlight Publishing Company ~ Sharing the Wisdom of the Stars, and Kona Bear Classics ~ Wise Words for Young Readers, and Founder/Hostess/Up-and-coming Blogger Incubator at: **www.CozyBySweetStarlight.com**, and **www.AstrologyKissedTravelBliss.com**

You can see more products and services offered by Annie Botticelli at: **www.AnnieHelpsYou.com** and her Youtube Channel at: **www.AnnieHelpsYouTV.com**

ALSO BY THE AUTHOR:

Tough Pill to Swallow

The Faerie Queen Chronicles ~ Book 1 ~ The Golden Gate

Principles of Empowerment for Relationships

You're Just Not Into You ~ Get Into Yourself and Change Your Life

More titles are being added regularly, check these links for updates:
www.AnnieHelpsYou.com/Books
www.LuminousLifeBooks.com
www.SweetStarlightBooks.com
www.KonaBearClassics.com

How to use this book

Let the magic of your intuition guide you to the best use of this book. I intentionally created 28 prayers as I am acutely aware of the power of doing things for 28 days in a row. It is said that it takes 28 days to make a new habit. This is not an arbitrary number as it is the approximate length of a moon cycle. Feel into doing one prayer for the whole 28 days or doing a different one each day. If staying consistent for the whole cycle doesn't call out to you now, then just use the prayers as it feels perfect for you. You may feel drawn to randomly open the book intending to land on the perfect prayer for you to work with and trusting Infinite Spirit to guide you. You can read the prayers quietly letting the words stay only in your mind, or you can say them out loud, knowing that voice often increases manifestation. Using the prayer mudra, holding this by your heart as you pray, can also add to the power of the prayers' manifestation. To amplify the effects of prayer you can tap on Emotional Freedom

Technique meridian tapping points while quietly reading each prayer or saying out loud. You can also take clips or phrases that have great resonance and hold them as mantras and repeat them out loud or quietly in your mind as affirmations. I have used many different names for the Infinite Source, you can use the ones I list or sub in whatever you are most comfortable calling the All-That-Is.

As we transform ourselves, so we transform the world.

Happy Praying!
Annie

1

THANK YOU, INFINITE
SOURCE, FOR GIVING ME
THE GRAND BLESSING
OF RAW AUTHENTICITY
TODAY.

Thank you, Infinite Source, for giving me the grand blessing of raw authenticity today. Goodness could I use some support saying NO when I mean NO! and saying YES when I mean YES! and for taking the time and space to figure things out when I am sitting in MAYBE. Thank you for helping me to do this! I am ready to be an even more powerful catalyst for radical positive change and to do this I know I have to be profoundly honest with myself and others, setting the model for those who are ready to dance on this path of empowerment. Today, with your help, I lovingly take back my life. Thank you for showing me the way to be a 'Healthy Boundary Setting Ninja', never missing a trick or an opportunity to add ebullient consciousness and buoyant vibrance back into my life, my daily dynamics, and my relationships. I claim this day as the day of my freedom.

I break loose!
I am free!

2

THANK YOU,
BENEVOLENT SOURCE,
FOR INSTILLING WITHIN
ME INFINITE PATIENCE
AND OVERRIDING
ACCEPTANCE AND
COMPASSION IN
AREAS OF MY LIFE
WHERE INTOLERANCE
PREVIOUSLY REIGNED.

Thank you, Benevolent Source, for instilling within me infinite patience and overriding acceptance and compassion in areas of my life where intolerance previously reigned. Thank you for helping me to use the power of my breath to spare my adrenals and my whole body, mind, and Spirit, the unnecessary work and drama of overreaction. Thank you for helping me notice right away when tightness comes to my solar plexus, that desire to control something that is out of my hands.

Thank you for helping me automatically return to my breath to keep space and flow in my diaphragm, in my life. In the cases where I have had too much patience, thank you for letting me see clearly and dissolve connections to the origins of this fear of setting healthy boundaries, this unwillingness to protect myself and others where it is my place. When I see injustice around me, please let me know clearly which things are mine to work with, to step in to defend. In the cases where it is not my place to interfere with another's journey, thank you for blessing me with certainty, direction, and peace about my place in the situation. In the circumstances where I discover that it is my behavior that requires shifting, thank you for helping me to be brave and loving at the same time. Thank you for helping me to make adjustments in an empowered way, without blame or judgment of self or the other party. Thank you for assisting me in focusing on the light in the situation and bringing light to the situation.

In cases where darkness is coming out of me, righteous or other anger, or other negative emotions, thank you for helping me be responsible with the release of these poisons so that I don't infect anyone or anything else with the venom of negativity. Thank you for letting me see feelings as my friends, not to be avoided, but also not to be inappropriately placed, or dwelled upon past their usefulness in healing. Thank you for aiding me in working out negative charge through productive means so that I serve as a force for transcendence in this wonderful world.

Thank you, Thank you, Thank you!

3

THANK YOU,
BENEVOLENT CREATOR/
CREATRIX, FOR HELPING
ME TO SEE THE WORLD
DIFFERENTLY TODAY.

Thank you, Benevolent Creator/Creatrix, for helping me to see the world differently today. In places where I was cynical or critical, please gift me the experience of transcendent peace. In places where I saw darkness, please instill in me understanding and hope.

In areas where I was charged with negativity, thank you for bringing in the light of Infinite awareness. Where I have had tunnel vision, please broaden my view to see the bigger picture.

Thank you for helping me understand the world as a magical playground of reflections and projections where understanding the rules of the Game, brings success and joy in the experience. Thank you for letting me see myself as the powerful Creatrix/Creator that I am. As I am a reflection of you, please help me understand my power. Thank you for assisting me in learning quickly when I get off track, and in doing the work necessary to use my power in the best ways.

Thank you for helping me see I am here to vibrantly and consciously create, and help me feel empowered in that role.

4

THANK YOU, SOURCE
OF ALL THINGS, FOR
HELPING ME TO SPARKLE
WITH CREATIVITY
TODAY.

Thank you, Source of All Things, for helping me to sparkle with creativity today. Thank you for assisting me in remembering that I am on this Earth plane to create and help me do that consciously today. Thank you for helping me to see clearly what I don't want, so that I have more power to align with what I do want. Thank for helping me to use the resources available to me to aid my magical creations. Help me catch myself the moment I start focusing unproductively on the things I don't want, and shift my vision and my emotions to align with my desire. Please help me keep in my consciousness at all times the remembrance that my feelings are one of my most powerful tools of creation. Please assist me in acknowledging feelings I have that are contrary to my vision, as I know that stuffing or avoiding negative feelings will only work against me, and instead of dwelling on the feeling unproductively, let me use my breath as negative emotions come up so that I bring space, flow, and light carried by breath to the muscle memory within me that is calling out to be acknowledged. Help me remember today and always that being with emotions through reconnecting to breath will serve to integrate the issues, whereas staying in negative emotion without conscious breathing will not access or clear the true origin of the issue. Thank you for assisting me in holding space for the younger version of myself that had needs unmet and feelings unfelt or unacknowledged, and then to return back to my conscious alignment with you for my Divine to-do list to implement in my exciting role as Co-Creator/ Creatrix with you. In cases where my role as a caretaker of others has muted my capacity to be in touch with my own desires, please let me see that. Thank you for helping me to make room for my own highest desires, knowing that as I follow that path I can show up better for others and also teach and inspire them to do the same.

Thank you for this magical day of conscious co-creation with you!

5

Thank you, Infinite Spirit, for helping me to be easy on myself today, and to be easier on others, to soften my opinions, leaving room for awareness of the other side of the polarities I am swinging between.

Thank you, Infinite Spirit, for helping me to be easy on myself today, and to be easier on others, to soften my opinions, leaving room for awareness of the other side of the polarities I am swinging between. Thank you for helping me to see clearly how judgement of any kind hurts myself and others, to see the tricks of the ego that look to make exceptions to this. Please let me see clearly how in an interconnected Universe, one judgement sets a ripple in motion that works against the joy you so deeply want us to experience. Please help me understand the difference between awareness and acknowledgement of an issue and staying stuck in the issue from the constant focus on it. Thank you for helping me to use the power of my senses to see, hear, smell, taste, dream awake, the wonderful reality I know is available to me.

Thank you,
Thank you,
Thank you!

DEAR INFINITE SPIRIT: THANK YOU FOR ASSISTANCE IN METICULOUSLY WATCHING MY WORDS TODAY, LETTING ME HEAR MYSELF CLEARLY.

DEAR INFINITE SPIRIT:

Thank you for assistance in meticulously watching my words today, letting me hear myself clearly. Please show me the word choices that are keeping me from experiencing more joy and help me to reprogram the deeply ingrained habitual tones of voice, and negative thoughts implied in speech but not communicated directly that are poisoning my life with dysfunction. Thank you for showing me the ways I can shift my speech, my viewpoints, my beliefs, my opinions, my words, my thoughts, to a vibration that helps lift all sentient beings into higher planes of existence. Thank you for helping me have more compassion for myself and others as I honestly assess my circumstances and to be brave as I choose the road less traveled, paving the way for others who boldly decide to traverse this same path. Please help my choices be a light to spark

Conscious Evolution for these daring few who desire to make the road less traveled the new norm. As I make different choices, please help me to not judge or look down on my former self before moving to this path, and please let me not look down on others still choosing different realities. Thank you for helping me to remember there is no 'right way' to find ones way to Spirit and let me look with awe and wonder as I travel, awake to the magic that is nearby and always accessible.

THANK YOU, INFINITE
CREATOR/CREATRIX,
FOR HELPING ME TO
REMEMBER TODAY THAT
THE MAGIC OF THE
UNSEEN REALMS IS REAL.

Thank you, Infinite Creator/Creatrix, for helping me to remember today that the magic of the unseen realms is REAL. In this Universe where it is measured that we are only 10-20% conscious of all the things that are present around us, that means there is 80-90% of truths in our experience that we have yet to discover, learn, remember. Thank you for helping me remember that just as not seeing with my own eyes how a cell phone or computer connects with others nearby and across the world doesn't negate the truth of it happening, so are there countless things that are going on away from my third dimensional vision that are truly happening. Thank you for helping me to consciously rely upon and actively draw upon the spheres of magical potential of the unseen realms as my new 'norm'.

Please help me remember that the more I work on the inner/lesser seen realms, the more the magic of these realms reveals itself to me. Thank you for helping me dive bravely into the ancient spiritual truths that supersede the limits and limitations of the third-dimensional reality and remember my multi-dimensionality as an all-prevailing truth. Thank you for helping me call upon the wizard within and become empowered with magic in new and wonderful ways.

Thank you,
thank you,
thank you!

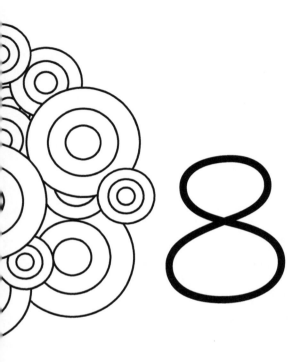

Gracious Creatrix/ Creator:
Thank you for helping me stay connected to you consciously at all times so that what I create can be in-line with your Will.

GRACIOUS CREATRIX/CREATOR:

Thank you for helping me stay connected to you consciously at all times so that what I create can be in-line with your Will. Thank you for helping me want what you want for me. Please help me understand the difference between My Will and Thy Will and willingly surrender over to ride the wave of your power through conscious alignment of my energy with the Divine Plan. Thank you for assisting me to consciously align My Will with that of the Divine making me an unstoppable force of Creation guaranteed to reach perfect ends. In places where I am in resistance, please let me recognize this and fill that tightness with lightness and limberness, ready to bend to your Will. Thank you for helping me to be a Spiritual Warrior, ready and equipped at each moment to recognize, own, and slay my dragons. Thank you for making sure I always remember that no matter how much my issues, challenges, and obstacles appear to be 'out there', they are actually 'in here', in my own being. Thank you for ensuring I always remember the source of my empowerment is in this awareness of my issues being housed within me and while sometimes it is appropriate to do work or tend to details outside of myself, the true work lies within.

Thank you,
Thank you,
Thank you!

THANK YOU,
BENEVOLENT CREATOR/
CREATRIX, FOR GIVING
ME THE GIFT OF
CONSTANT GRATITUDE
TODAY, FOR LIGHTING
EACH MOMENT WITH
THE REMEMBRANCE OF
THE MIRACLE OF EACH
PERSON, PLACE, AND
THING I SEE, I FEEL, I
EXPERIENCE IN THIS
MAGICAL WORLD.

Thank you, Benevolent Creator/Creatrix, for giving me the gift of constant gratitude today, for lighting each moment with the remembrance of the miracle of each person, place, and thing I see, I feel, I experience in this magical world. Thank you for letting me bring pillowy cushions to the hard edges I come across today, for helping me acknowledge each person, animal, thing, location, circumstance as the magical wonder it is. Thank you for helping me to bring conscious awareness of the fragility of life and the importance of this moment. Thank you for assisting me to balance future planning and past recollections with generous doses of all-encompassing acceptance of and relishing in the delicious here and now.

Thank you,
Thank you,
Thank you!

THANK YOU, INFINITE
SOURCE, FOR HELPING
ME TO BRING MORE
COHERENCE TO MY
SURROUNDINGS TODAY.

Thank you, Infinite Source, for helping me to bring more coherence to my surroundings today. Please help me readily recognize how clutter and disorganization in my external space negatively affects my inner space and spur me to action on this today. Thank you for helping me to make progress today, however small, in clearing out and better organizing my personal space. Thank you for helping me to clear the easy things that have no emotional charge so that I feel like I am making progress and so that I create more space and coherence that will help me in dealing with the things that are harder to clear through. Thank you for helping me to attract resources, support, and determination, to shift my surroundings into as much beauty and coherence as I can and that feels good to create, at this time. Thank you for helping me create systems that work for my daily flow. Please infuse me with ingenuity and resourcefulness that makes the creation of these systems easy and fun. Thank you for sharpening my discernment so that I stop the issues of clutter and disorganization at their point of entry, instead of wasting time letting so much in then having to do the work to clear it out. I ask for your assistance in helping me to stop and feel in before I bring more things into my space so that I carefully discern whether it is beneficial for me to invite each item in. Please help me to also have the same discernment with people, experiences, and other decisions. Thank you for helping me to own my energy field and tend to it with great meticulousness and joy.

I am excited for this great day of releasing things that no longer serve me and I welcome into this newly created space, amazing experiences, warm support, and sparkly opportunities for wonderful things that really resonate with this new version of myself being birthed.

I am so grateful for your help, guidance, and support.

Thank you,

Thank you,

Thank you!

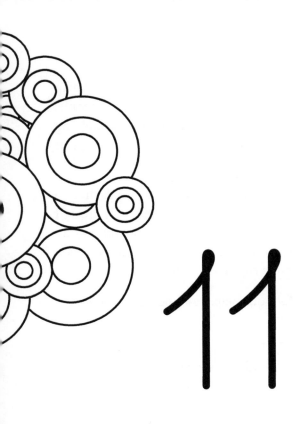

11

THANK YOU, INFINITE
SPIRIT, FOR GIVING
ME PATIENCE WITH
THE SHORTCOMINGS I
PERCEIVE IN OTHERS.

Thank you, Infinite Spirit, for giving me patience with the shortcomings I perceive in others. Thank you for helping me see the reflections others offer me through how I feel about these perceptions. Please shine the light of awareness on me when I need help remembering or understanding that when someone or something 'upsets' me, it is a cue to become aware that the event occurring is not the real issue, but instead to focus on the feeling I have from what happens, as that is showing the underlying imprint of core patterns I have had since childhood. Thank you for helping me to stay present in the feelings and not get swept away by the drama and the 'story' I create about what is happening. Please give me strength to empower myself by staying radically honest with myself about my circumstances, and owning the challenging experiences instead of falling into the trap of blame, shame, and guilt. Thank you for helping me become aware when I am pointing to the

origin of my issues as being outside of me, that there is a true starting point inside of me, and that I am the common denominator in my experience. Thank you for helping me always remember that true empowerment lies in the radical owning of my story as coming from within. As I remember this truth, I feel the true power I have to perfectly and permanently change my external situations to match my radical internal shifts.

Thank you,
thank you,
thank you!

THANK YOU, INFINITE
SPIRIT, FOR INFUSING
MY DAY, MY LIFE,
MY WORLD, WITH
POSITIVITY, HOPE,
AND FAITH.

Thank you, Infinite Spirit, for infusing my day, my life, my world, with positivity, hope, and faith. Thank you for helping me remember that even when things feel at their worst, good news, good luck, a magical breakthrough, or a major shift can happen at any time and that my positive anticipation of this shift can herald its appearance. Please help me to live in constant expectation of your Benevolence. Thank you for helping me be a light onto others that need some help and for making me magnetic to those who would be a light for me when I need it. I so appreciate you reminding me readily how miracles can show up at any time, and how the more I tap into this 'Miracle Vibration', the more I can powerfully attract miraculous events and outcomes.

Please help me break the addiction of worry, fear, and doubt, by retraining myself with diligent practice to stop in my tracks when I start to go along a negative mental path and make a rapid shift back into an upward spiral. Thank you for helping me to have a list of things that help to shift my vibe ready for these times when I am most vulnerable. Thank you for helping me to look for and find resources to support me in this quest for defiant optimism and actually use resources I have available to me to support this mission.

I can feel transformation crackling in my being and I wait with excited anticipation for the positive changes I know are brewing to make their way into wonderful and quick manifestation.

Thank you,
thank you!

13

THANK YOU, ALL-THAT-IS, FOR HELPING ME TO MASTER MONEY AND THE MATERIAL REALM.

Thank you, All-That-Is, for helping me to master money and the material realm. Thank you for blessing me with financial discernment and the gift of always living within my means. Please help me to always remember that money is neither good nor bad, it is simply energy, just like everything else in this wonderful world. I ask for help to locate and clear my judgements about money so that I can enter a new paradigm of greater ease with money and amazing prosperity far beyond anything I have ever experienced, or could previously imagine. Thank you for the pouring in of information, resources, and insights about money that allows me to break free from previous limitations. Thank you for opening my mind to new ways to attract and use money. Thank you for helping me to invest in my two greatest resources of all, myself and my connection with the Divine. Thank you for helping me to invest in, believe in, and fully utilize my own creative resourcefulness. Please give me the confidence I need to take the necessary steps to create a new financial reality for myself. Please assist those who can help me, to really see me and my work so that my gifts can be brought to light and acknowledged in greater ways. Thank you for helping me bring all the light I can muster to my perfect life's work that helps the world and helps me financially care for myself and my loved ones. Please let me live in gratitude and trust, focusing equally on honoring myself and where I am at and also what else I have to do to further expand. Thank you for assisting me in translating my gifts and hard work into a greater financial experience which I honor with good choices. I relish in your assistance in helping me live super-charged with excitement about the epic financial miracles in store for me.

I feel awe-inspiring news and sizzling breakthroughs popping through the surface of my experience, about to be readily visible in my life, and I am so grateful.

I OFFER MY GRATITUDE TODAY, INFINITE CREATOR/CREATRIX, FOR YOUR ASSISTANCE IN INCREASING MY EMOTIONAL IQ.

I offer my gratitude today, Infinite Creator/Creatrix, for your assistance in increasing my emotional IQ. Thank you for helping me to bring cardinal compassion to myself and others. Thank you for helping me to bring impeccable consciousness to my words and how they affect others and for continuing to search for methods of expression that honor myself and others and create win-win's. Thank you for helping me notice when I am overwhelmed and need some alone time. I ask for your assistance to help me get in the habit of taking some quiet personal time before I make commitments or agreements and before I engage on a topic that feels 'charged' or in other ways stressful to me. Please help me to take the time to feel while also not getting lost in my feelings and losing my power to the 'story'. Thank you for helping me to readily lift the judgment about feeling and to give myself and others the time needed to process through charged emotions. Please assist me in always tuning in to how it must feel to be in the other persons shoes, so that my capacity for compassion can be infinitely expanded. Instead of taking offense if I feel judged or criticized by someone, please help me to ask the empowering questions, "In what ways is this other person also 'right'?" and "What can I learn from this?"

Thank you for helping me to be infinitely patient with myself and others while also using great and growing discernment to continue moving along the upward spiral of Conscious Evolution.

15

THANK YOU, INFINITE
BENEVOLENT FORCE,
FOR HELPING ME TO
CAREFULLY EVALUATE
THE TOPIC OF FREEDOM.

Thank you, Infinite Benevolent Force, for helping me to carefully evaluate the topic of freedom. Please clearly show me the ways that I have held myself prisoner with belief systems that do not serve my Highest Expression. Thank you for helping me always remember that manifestation starts with imagination. Even if circumstances look completely hopeless, I can always count on the power of my imagination to conjure options that weren't readily available before. Thank you for helping me to remember that my subconscious mind can't tell the difference between a visualization and 'reality' and that with my diligent and consistent use of the power of my mind, I can show this faithful servant what ends I wish to reach and set it to work on the creation of my brilliant vision.

Please assist me in reframing the idea of freedom into those aspects of the experience I already enjoy. What I focus on, I create, so the more I feel the freedom that is my truth, the more this freedom pervades my experience.

Thank you for helping me to create wisely, manifest compassionately, and use my limitless creative faculties as a force for good in this wondrous world.

16

THANK YOU, INFINITE
SPIRIT, FOR HELPING
ME TO BECOME MORE
IN TOUCH WITH
NATURE AND NATURAL
RHYTHMS.

Thank you, Infinite Spirit, for helping me to become more in touch with nature and natural rhythms. Thank you for helping me to hold in my visceral remembrance that there are rhythms and cycles at play in every seen and unseen aspect of life and that the more I consciously sync up my personal Will with these, the more smoothly I can flow with the magic of life. Please help me do at least one thing every day that honors my personal circadian rhythm, like going to sleep when I am tired, going to sleep at close to the same time every day, waking up at the same time every day, watching the Sun set, watching the Sun rise, and anything else that consciously links me to the magical ebb and flow of Universal life force energy.

Thank you for assisting me to build daily rituals that support my reunion with the natural flow, including going outside every day, barefoot when possible, and putting my hands and third eye up to a tree or down to the Earth. When I lose my certainty, my footing, or feel the incoherent energies of phones, computers, TV's, "Smart meters", or routers taking over my energy field and my life, please help me to hear the wisdom of Nature and the Elements beckoning me back out to connect with sanity and coherence that is the answer to all my ails. Thank you for giving me daily awareness of how my surroundings are effecting the orb of energy around me that is the extension of myself, my electromagnetic field, my Aura.

Thank you for helping me learn and practice impeccable emotional, mental, physical, spiritual, and energetic hygiene as my awesome new daily experience.

Thank you, Infinite Creator/Creatrix, for expanding my awareness of my multi-dimensional experience and for helping me develop my psychic awareness, easily attracting and utilizing information and other tools to fine-tune my extra-sensory perceptions.

Thank you, Infinite Creator/Creatrix, for expanding my awareness of my multi-dimensional experience and for helping me develop my psychic awareness, easily attracting and utilizing information and other tools to fine-tune my extra-sensory perceptions. Thank you for also assisting me to equally increase my psychic protection rituals to safeguard myself and to use my expanding gifts with great and growing discernment. As the worlds of the lesser seen open up to me, thank you for helping me to always be grounded, having a solid footing in the 3-D reality so that I may function optimally in this experience as I expand and also for helping me to use my spiritual connections and awarenesses to help myself and others better understand the laws that govern our Earthly experience so that we can play the Game of Life in easier and more fulfilling ways. Thank you for helping me to perfectly balance ethereal and esoteric wisdom with practical mundane and worldly functionality. Please assist in making the upgrade process of all of my physical and subtle bodies be graceful and easy. I ask with loving gratitude to beam even more of your luminous truth and exhilarating vibrance out into the world in ways that enrich my experience and that of others.

Thank you,
Thank you,
Thank you!

THANK YOU, GOLDEN SOURCE, FOR HELPING ME TO CLEAR THE BELIEF IN AND EXPERIENCE OF DEBT.

Thank you, Golden Source, for helping me to clear the belief in and experience of debt. Please help me remember that as long as I think someone owes me something, because we live in a holographic reality, it will increase the odds that someone will be thinking I owe them something. Thank you for helping me remember that believing in the Victim/Tyrant polarity perpetuates the experience of debt and thank you for helping me clear this paradigm. Please help me forgive myself and others in deeper ways, on every level of my being. I know by offering others a true 'clean slate', that I am more likely to experience this myself. Thank you for the inpouring of resources and insights to help me on this journey of radical forgiveness. Please help me to see clearly how on some level I chose my parents, family, and other experiences, and as such, anything that has happened has been by 'Divine Design'. Thank you for helping me to bless, dismiss, and forgive these messengers that have seemed to bring me challenges, and embrace the lessons and growth that have come from the experiences. Please help me strip away judgments of people and circumstances, knowing that as I judge, I activate the blame, shame, and guilt cycle that keeps us all trapped.

Thank you for giving me freedom from this cycle and transcendence into trust and gratitude for the wisdom of the Divine Plan.

THANK YOU, GOLDEN
INFINITE SOURCE, FOR
HELPING ME TO REVEL
IN SCINTILLATING
SENSUAL DELIGHTS THAT
EXPAND MY HIGHEST
GOOD!

Thank you, Golden Infinite Source, for helping me to revel in scintillating sensual delights that expand my Highest Good! Thank you for helping me to create amazing new patterns where my indulgences are those that serve my Highest Good rather than work against it. Thank you for helping me eradicate addictions and step into radical self-love, profound self-care, and phenomenal self-appreciation, so all-encompassing that I only want to ingest the things that both bring me radiant joy to consume, and are also supremely supportive of my energy and systems on every level, honoring the dazzling Divinity that lies within my luminous sacred body temple. Thank you for helping me to be a magnet for those things that will fit this description and step into delightful new discoveries of superbly healthy sensory delights. Please help me to eat slowly with major mindfulness, allowing my food to completely digest and creating the space for me to carefully tune into how each bite feels in my body.

Thank you for helping me to befriend myself and beautiful body and the splendid foods and drinks that will support me in attaining and maintaining vibrant health and lively wellness.

DEAREST BENEVOLENT ONE: THANK YOU FOR MAKING THIS A DAY OF ASTONISHING MIRACLES.

Dearest Benevolent One:

Thank you for making this a day of astonishing miracles. Thank for helping me to see the dazzling truth of the holographic reality today ~ The Universal Principle of 'As Above, So Below ~ As Below, So Above' permeating my conscious awareness. Please help me to hold this magnificent truth in my consciousness as I walk through each day, applying it constantly and consistently to everything I see, knowing that every diligent moment I spend on notably raising my vibration, I am also simultaneously positively changing the world. Thank you for helping me to boldly and boisterously take on being the change that I want to see in the world. In places where I see discouraging lack of integrity in the world and feel angry about it, thank you for helping me to look for more ways for live in deeper and awe-inspiring integrity. When I see darkness in the world, please help me to own the conscious and unconscious shadows within me so that rather than judging what I see, I am accountable for my role in the current reflections. Thank you for helping me to faultlessly forgive myself and others as I see lower level vibrations rolling through me and around me. Please bless me with industrious impeccability, so that I can steadfastly apply this lens of spiritual truth always, and in the cases where I don't lead with Spirit, thank you for helping me to always return to the Spiritual view and path with renewed effervescence.

I am sorry,
please forgive me,
thank you,
I love you.

21

THANK YOU,
BENEVOLENT DIVINE
CREATRIX/CREATOR,
FOR LIFTING ALL THE
CELLS IN MY BODY WITH
THIS TRANSCENDENT
KNOWING ~ MONEY
COMES DIRECTLY
FROM SPIRIT.

Thank you, Benevolent Divine Creatrix/Creator, for lifting all the cells in my body with this transcendent knowing ~ MONEY COMES DIRECTLY FROM SPIRIT. Thank you for helping me to remember that I am not limited by what my employer, spouse, parents, or any other source is giving me, and that I can bypass the belief that the 'middleman' holds the key to my income, asking for my prosperity directly from the Divine Ethers. Eternal thanks for helping me establish right now, growing every day, this foundation of unwavering trust in the Infinite, anchored by the zealous commitment to do the inner work it takes to move mountains around me. Thank you for helping me to say YES to powerful daily practices that shift my inner paradigms to ones that attract money to me in wonderful ways and also simultaneously say YES to establishing and enthusiastically enforcing the discernment it takes to manage money in a way that ensures my fabulous financial freedom.

I look so forward to your help in establishing the unshakeable inner security that is necessary to the experience of stable outer security.

Thank you for this glowing feeling of inner and outer certainty that has become my new norm.

I see and feel into creation, being wrapped warm and cozy, in lush material and plush emotional comfort.

THANK YOU, INFINITE
SOURCE OF LIGHT,
FOR LEADING ME TO
THE PERFECT DIET,
SUPPLEMENTS, AND
LIFESTYLE THAT SERVE
MY BODY, MIND,
AND SPIRIT.

Thank you, Infinite Source of Light, for leading me to the perfect diet, supplements, and lifestyle that serve my body, mind, and Spirit. Thank you for helping me to be an Intuitarian, to eat, drink, take in, participate in the foods, drinks, and activities that serve my Highest Expression at all times. In places where I am confused about what my body wants or needs, please let me have more clarity to best implement the best case scenarios for my life. Thank you for bringing me the perfect practitioners, spiritual and other practices, highest vibrational sustenance, that makes my soul sing and my body vibrate with radiance. Thank you for bringing to my awareness all of the situations, dynamics, and beliefs, that brought my current level of health and vitality, and for helping me be strong and disciplined in doing the necessary work. In cases where my discipline needs more flexibility, help me see that and see clearly how I can make shifts to allow for more magic, flow, and enjoyment in my life. In cases where I have to let certain foods, drinks, habits, lifestyles, go, please help me to know that through the sadness and confusion of the transition, that I can be confident that I am headed to higher ground, and that things will get easier for me on this path. Thank you for shifting my points of resonance away from things that work against me and towards things that fill me with more light. Thank you for helping me not to buy into beliefs and practices, just because others believe in them, but instead let me be led by Spirit, through awareness, intuition, and synchronicity, to the ways of being that are right for me at any given time. As I make these changes, please help me to not become so rigid in my belief about them, that I lose connection to the constant and ever-changing communications of my body, which will keep me on track. Please let me be flexible enough in my beliefs to always remember that there can be more than one 'right' way. Please let me remember that everyone has their own journey and that what is right for me, may not be right for someone else. In cases where I am drawn to share about my experience, please let my words carry the truth of my knowing that there are many paths to wellness, and that my way is not an absolute. Thank you for my optimum wellness of body, mind, and Spirit and for helping me to LOVE... ACCEPT... CHERISH... ADORE my Body Temple... and always remember the DIVINITY it houses.

THANK YOU, SAGE SOURCE, FOR HELPING ME TO EMBRACE THE UNKNOWN WITH THE SPIRIT OF A GREAT ADVENTURER!

Thank you, Sage Source, for helping me to embrace the unknown with the spirit of a great adventurer! Thank you for helping me adjust my viewpoint to remember that each new turn on my path can yield amazing discoveries and awesome experiences. Thank you for helping me to reframe the unknown as the bringer of delightful potentials and to welcome change as it comes without resistance. Please help me greet new experiences as I do that first cool day in late summer, with refreshing relief, and as I do the first bud of spring popping through the last snow, with smiling expectation, feeling the warm promise of Spring's abundance of color and scent. Thank you for helping me to experience each day as a brilliant new and clean slate, holding as a comforting hug the lessons and wisdom from the past, pressed next to the peace of the present moment, wrapped tight with the awe of the magic yet to come.

Thank you,
Thank you,
Thank you!

THANK YOU, DIVINE
SPIRIT, FOR HELPING
ME TO BE BRAVE
AND THROW MYSELF
HEADLONG IN THE
DIRECTION OF MY
DREAMS.

Thank you, Divine Spirit, for helping me to be brave and throw myself headlong in the direction of my dreams. I am so grateful for your help in remembering my power and using it to VIBRATE LOUDLY WITH MY MAGICAL HEARTSONG. Thank you for helping me to remember and own my unique purpose in this beautiful world. In cases where I am not clear about my way, thank you for sending trustworthy messengers with clear information to help me get back on track. Thank you for helping me to become acutely aware of sleeping and waking dreams and synchronicities that are occurring to put me on or get me back on my path. Once I gain clarity, thank you for helping me to have the diligent discipline I need to carry through my Divine instructions for bringing my Light out into the world in growing ways. Thank you for helping me remember that I can succeed in life not from lack of fear but in spite of it. Fear often shows me what is standing between me and my Highest Destiny. Thank you for helping me to discern between fear that is genuinely led from intuition as a protection measure and fear that is a block to work through. I so appreciate you giving me the tools and wherewithal to both honor intuitive messages to step back and wait and to blast through fear that is no longer serving me, easily seeing when each is appropriate. Thank you for helping me to see that true power comes not from avoiding but instead owning the darkness within me and using it as alchemical fuel to create the golden vibration of transcendent joy.

Thank you for helping me to be a Spiritual Ninja, stealthily moving through the darkness and boldly stepping into brilliant dawn, the life of my dreams, and my Highest Expression, and to inspire others to do the same.

THANK YOU, DIVINE
LIGHT, FOR HELPING
ME TO REMEMBER THE
LIMITLESS POTENTIAL
OF ALL THAT IS AND TO
TAKE THAT EXPANSIVE
KNOWING WITH ME
THROUGHOUT THIS DAY.

Thank you, Divine Light, for helping me to remember the limitless potential of all that is and to take that expansive knowing with me throughout this day. Where I encounter limitations and restrictions, let me remember that in an Infinite Reality, there are infinite outcomes, infinite solutions to what may appear to be a 'problem'. Also, please help me remember that what seems like a 'problem' is often an opportunity in disguise. Please let me see clearly how obstacles can serve as springboards for my magnificent creations and deepest fulfillment. Thank for helping me remember that pressure or challenge can serve as a catalyst to break out of the matrix of one reality and into a whole new and better experience. Thank you for helping me to reframe problems as messengers, friends sent to me to help me see where I am at in my work and what next I am to do.

Thank you for helping me add to issues that come up the alchemical ingredients of my accountability and perspective and create gold from lead. Thank you for helping me to become a master "lemonade-maker" when life gives me lemons. I am ever grateful for your guidance to help me to hold in my being the truth that behind, above, below, and woven through everything is your Golden Benevolence. I am so grateful for my ever-growing ability to see the "glass as half-full" and the part that is empty as also being FULL, of ENDLESS POSSIBILITIES for DELICIOUS AWESOMENESS. I dance in limitless potential and co-create the most ecstatic manifestations.

THANK YOU, GOLDEN
SOURCE, FOR HELPING
ME BE AN IRRESISTIBLE
MAGNET FOR AWESOME
EXPERIENCES, JOYFULLY
ACCEPTING IN A FRENZY
OF FUN AND CRAZY
AMOUNTS OF HIGH VIBE
FROLIC INTO MY LIFE.

Thank you, Golden Source, for helping me be an irresistible magnet for awesome experiences, joyfully accepting in a FRENZY of FUN and crazy amounts of High Vibe frolic into my life. Thank you for weaving awareness and discernment into these choices and experiences. I am so grateful that in having fun I set myself free, bring in balance, and inspire others to do the same. Thank you for helping me to remember that fun is a necessary part of life, just as water and air are. I delight in letting my inner child be footloose and fancy free and I know that the more I do this, the more creative genius in the form of ideas, solutions, and other manifestations will be powerfully drawn to me.

Thank you,
Thank you,
Thank you!

Thank you, Wise Source, for helping me see and feel into creation being surrounded by deep comfort and love by first establishing deep love and security within myself and certainty in my constant connection to the Benevolent and Infinite Source.

Thank you, Wise Source, for helping me see and feel into creation being surrounded by deep comfort and love by first establishing deep love and security within myself and certainty in my constant connection to you, the Benevolent and Infinite Source. Thank you for helping me to easily pull from the closet of the Golden Ethers the softest, coziest, most comfortable blanket I could imagine and feel it wrapped tightly around me when I need a reminder of the consistent ethereal support that is always available to me, even when, and especially when, the material world is not being so forthcoming with comfort.

I know that in an ever-changing world, the only constant I can count on is the concrete anchor of the Divine and the more I focus on this steadfast safeguard of Spirit, the more I can bring that sureness into each day in the material realm that is so full of dizzying change. I know that the antidote to the relentless uncertainty of the mundane reality is taking the time to build and maintain my conscious connection to the Ballast of the Benevolent.

Thank you for assisting me in this daily mission to prioritize my awareness of my continual access to this solid Golden Force of Good, this Perpetual Pillar of Power that is the All-That-Is.

THANK YOU, INFINITE
WONDER, FOR BLESSING
ME TODAY AND EVERY
DAY WITH DEFIANT
OPTIMISM AND
RELENTLESS HOPE.

Thank you, Infinite Wonder, for blessing me today and every day with defiant optimism and relentless hope. I know that the vibration of positivity serves as a beacon for sparkling outcomes and I want to be a light of emphatic certainty. Please let me lead with my sure heart today and in instances where I slip into fear or negativity, thank you for hastening my return to Spirit's silver lining. Thank you for granting me eager readiness to find solutions today and to be a powerful force that gently defuses charge around me assisting in bringing peace to the world, one interaction at a time. Please help me to create consistency in starting my day out and ending each day with prayer and gratitude. I am so grateful for the gift of infusion with confidence in myself, in my Divine Plan, in life.

I can feel the wings of my true freedom being attained while still in physical form stretching further every day. I revel in this experience of glorious transcendence that allows me to BE in the world but not be of it. I relish in the juicy balance of owning my perfect humanity at the same time as my flawless Divinity. Thank you for blessing me with the awareness of constant connection to everyone, everything, all that is, all that was, and all that ever will be at the same time as acknowledging, owning, sharing, and rocking my brilliant individuality, bringing to the world what only I can bring.

I start this day and finish this day with a big smile ready to do what I came here to do - be the Awesome, Incredible, Brilliantly-Shining, Ever-Evolving ME.

Lightning Source UK Ltd.
Milton Keynes UK
UKHW021523041219
354706UK00011B/2770/P